MW00568497

...o down, as you've contemplated the birds who share your environment so near and yet so far and unattainable, you've dreamed of spreading your own wings, of soaring, of letting the wind lift you far into the sky, o ethereal routes free of any obstacle, on routes providing a magnificent view of all of earth's countless beauties. What a wonderful dream

most wondrous and beautiful creatures on our planet. We look at them or the pleasure they bring to our eyes, we study them to understand their behavior, we use them as a source of inspiration to reach higher, to each further. It comes as no surprise that birds have inspired so very many of our poets and song writers. Words and lyrics that speak of

o doubt, as you've contemplated the birds who share your environment
ear and yet so far and unattainable, you've dreamed of spreading y
wn wings, of soaring, of letting the wind lift you far into the sky, on ether
l routes free of any obstacle, on routes providing a magnificent view of
f earth's countless beauties. What a wonderful dream! What a wond
ul sense of weightlessness! What wonderful freedom! From the tin
ummingbird to the mightiest eagle, from the brightest plumed to the maj
cally black birds are among the most wondrous and beautiful creatu

n o
tud
aspi
irds
nd
um
on's
ust
ighe
unu
eartl
plate
unal
ettin
le, e
es..

What wonderful freedom! From the tiniest hummingbird to the might
eagle, from the brightest plumed to the majestically black, birds are am
he most wondrous and beautiful creatures on our planet. We look
hem for the pleasure they bring to our eyes, we study them to underst
heir behavior, we use them as a source of inspiration to reach highe
each further. It comes as no surprise that birds have inspired so
many of our poets and song writers. Words and lyrics that speak
light are common in every human language. The human's longin

Garden of
Birds

This book belongs to

© 2000 Modus Vivendi Publishing Inc.
All rights reserved.

Published by:
Modus Vivendi Publishing Inc.
3859 Laurentian Autoroute
Laval, Quebec
Canada H7L 3H7
or
2565 Broadway, Suite 161
New York, New York 10025

Translation: Brenda O'Brien
Cover: Marc Alain

Picture Credits: © Digital Vision and SuperStock

Legal Deposit: 3rd Quarter, 2000
National Library of Canada

Canadian Cataloguing in Publication Data
Therrien, Laurette
    Garden of Birds
    (Heartfelt Series)
    Translation of: Jardin d'oiseaux.
    ISBN: 2-89523-025-0
    1. Birds. 2. Birds – Pictorial works. I. Title. II. Series
QL673.T4313 2000   598   C00941191-7

        We acknowledge the financial support of the Government
of Canada through the Book Publishing Industry Development
Program (BPIDP) for our publishing activities.

Garden of
Birds

Laurette Therrien

MV Publishing

Flight:
The Ultimate Dream

No doubt, as you've contemplated the birds who share your environment, so near and yet so far and unattainable, you've dreamed of spreading your own wings, of soaring, of letting the wind lift you far into the sky, on ethereal routes free of any obstacle, on routes providing a magnificent view of all of earth's countless beauties. What a wonderful dream! What a wonderful sense of weightlessness! What wonderful freedom!

From the tiniest hummingbird to the mightiest eagle, from the brightest plumed to the majestically black, birds are among the most wondrous and beautiful creatures on our planet. We look at them for the pleasure they bring to our eyes, we study them to understand their behavior, we use them as a source of inspiration to reach higher, to reach further.

It comes as no surprise that birds have inspired so very many of our poets and song writers. Words and lyrics that speak of flight are common in every human language. The human fascination with winged creatures is universal. Almost every person's fantasies include the dream of taking flight.

We invite you to do just that as you read the following pages. They will definitely take you higher and further; they will help you soar above everyday worries, life's mundane obstacles and its major challenges; they will lift from your earthbound shoulders the weight of the world.

L.T.

A Bird in the Hand

I

They had been invited to a celebration marking the birthday of the Cardinal, alias the Grand Duke of Mongolia. The party was an idea spawned by Claudia, a **pigeon-chested** young lady, a slightly **feather-brained** girl, known for her many **flights of fancy**. She had many friends and she loved their company. The more, the merrier. Her friends, all of whom were friends of the Cardinal as well, were from the artistic world and on this particular day, they willingly came out to celebrate; the bad weather was like **water off a duck's back** to them. And so since a **bird in the hand is worth two in the bush**, they set aside many another invitation in favour of an evening in the Petit Coq restaurant, a French establishment renowned for its absolutely divine confit of fatted goose.

At the very end of the long line of guests was an extremely tall and emaciated gentlemen, very **stork-like** and **eagle-nosed**, someone who usually looked **mad as a wet hen**. A polyglot, the man liked to taunt his fellow diners and would often bombastically boast that he could **sing like a lark**. On this particular occasion he was in the company of a younger man, known for his penchant for **robin's egg blue**, but today decked out in **canary** yellow, a curious colour to choose for a **swallow-tailed** coat. The darling of every older woman in the group, he was known for his ability to **charm the birds out of the trees**.

Come from home, almost fifty miles away **as the crow flies**, the two were a most peculiar duo.

(to be continued)

A Bird in the Hand

II

Just ahead of them, an **odd goose**, teetering on very high-heeled shoes, kept **parroting** that **one swallow doesn't make a summer**, a saying she had picked up on her last foray into aristocratic circles. Her companion, decked out in an eye-catchingly short dress, was gossiping and sharing tales that a **little bird told her**, in the meantime complaining that the weather was so bitter she had permanent **goosebumps**. Her rumours seemed to be of great interest to her nearest neighbour, a fat little **penguin**, every bit as supercilious as his interlocutor, proving that **birds of a feather flock together**.

Eyeing the crowd like a **vulture**, his attitude came as no surprise to anyone. He was widely known to be **as jealous as a pigeon**, as everyone could attest, and his current worry was his spouse's keen interest in the **cock of the walk**, a **strange bird** and a regular hanger-on at these events.

No **lame duck**, our Lothario was busy inviting Madame to his **love nest**, and, preening like a **lovebird**, she certainly showed no hesitation — on the contrary, she seemed ready to **spread her wings and fly**. Some onlookers later claimed that they were planning a day of **skylarking**.

(to be continued)

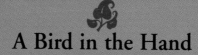

A Bird in the Hand

III

The brouhaha came to an abrupt end as Claudia made her appearance, scanning the group like a watchman in **a crow's nest**, prancing about, eager to let potential suitors know that she was **free as a bird**. In a gown designed to show off her beautiful **swan neck**, she haughtily announced:

"My dear friends, the Cardinal will not be joining us tonight. Unfortunately, ever since he met Lady Finch, **a goose that lays the golden eggs** as far as he is concerned, he is given to **flights of fancy**! A chatterbox, as you all know, she likes **to make the feathers fly**. Her company will not be missed. Our beloved Cardinal has become **proud as a peacock** and is offended that our celebration will not take place at the Ritz!"

"He can well **swan about**," said the **stork-like** guest, in tones best kept for someone who fancies himself **a wise old owl**, "she'll soon be **sharpening her beak** at his expense."

A tad insulted, the guests began to mill around, debating on whether it was worth while staying. Eventually **getting their hackles up**, the ladies on hand **trilled** that they didn't need the Cardinal after all. In fact, he tended **to chatter like a magpie**. But Claudia bid them to be quiet: "My fine guests, Chef **Featherstone** has prepared a meal fit for a king. I urge you to take your seats and prepare for a feast."

"No need **to set the cat among the pigeons**," chimed in a lady dressed in a **flamingo-pink** shawl. "After all, **a bird in the hand is worth two in the bush**."

(to be continued)

A Bird in the Hand

IV

The meal was memorable. The Cardinal's absence was soon forgotten and each course was warmly applauded. The menu included many a dish, and not one complaint was heard throughout the evening, only songs of praise:

- Divine confit of fatted goose, a specialty patented by Chef Featherstone.
- Swallow's nest soup, a dish borrowed from the Far East.
- Duck in orange sauce, complemented by salted and marinated algae.
- Quail's eggs stuffed with turkey breast.
- A duo of nightingale and skylark eggs.
- Partridge stuffed with raisins and rosemary.
- Oriole hearts sautéed in red wine.
- Roast pheasant Madagascar-style, on a bed of mushrooms and chestnuts.
- Chicken livers in Malmsey wine.

Unfortunately, Chef Featherstone refused to share his recipes with us — the sole exception: Chicken Livers in Malmsey Wine, a dish he created specifically for the Cardinal, alias Grand Duke of Mongolia, whose affront he has never accepted. Indeed, the insult gave rise to a definite fallout and a genuine **cockfight** some seven or eight days later. But that's a whole other story.

ANDIGENA LAMINIROSTRIS Gould

Chicken Livers
in Malmsey Wine

- 2 lbs/1 kg fresh chicken livers
- 2 tablespoons butter
- 2 tablespoons olive oil
- 3 tablespoons flour
- 2 cups/500 ml defatted chicken broth
- 1 large onion, finely chopped
- 2 cloves garlic, minced
- 1/4 cup/25 g flat-leaved parsley, chopped
- salt and freshly ground pepper
- a pinch of thyme
- 1/2 cup/125 ml of Malmsey or Madeira wine

1. Wash and pat the chicken livers dry.
2. Heat the butter and olive oil together and sauté the chicken livers over high heat, approximately 5 minutes, turning only once.
3. Remove the livers and keep warm.
4. Add the flour to the butter mixture remaining in the pan and cook for 1 minute, stirring with a wooden spoon.
5. Add the chicken broth; stir constantly, until the sauce thickens.
6. Add the onion, garlic, parsley, salt and pepper and thyme; let simmer for 3 minutes, stirring.
7. Add the Malmsey wine and let simmer 5 minutes more.
8. Add the chicken livers to the sauce; serve with rice and a green vegetable.

Liver is very rich in iron, but don't worry, it's good for you and it definitely won't make you feather-brained! Enjoy!

Rain and the Robin

A robin in the morning,
In the morning early,
Sang a song of warning,
"There'll be rain, there'll be rain."
Very, very clearly
From the orchard
Came the gentle horning,
"There'll be rain."
But the hasty farmer
Cut his hay down,
Did not heed the charmer
From the orchard,
And the mower's clatter
Ceased at noontide,
For with drip and spatter
Down came the rain.
Then the prophet robin
Hidden in the crab-tree
Railed upon the farmer,
"I told you so, I told you so."
As the rain grew stronger,
And his heart grew prouder,
Notes so full and slow
Coming blither, louder,
"I told you so, I told you so,
"I told you so."

Duncan Campbell Scott
(1862-1947)

The tiniest living thing
That soars on feathered wing,
Or crawls among the long grass out of sight
Has just as good a right
To its appointed portion of delight
As any King.

Christina Rossetti

Hail, Bishop Valentine, whose day this is:
All the air is thy diocese,
And all the chirping choristers
And other birds are thy parishioners:
Thou marriest every year
The lyric lark and the grave whispering dove,
The sparrow that neglects his life for love,
The household bird with the red stomacher.

John Donne

To all the humble beasts there be,
To all the birds on land and sea,
Great Spirit! sweet protection give,
That free and happy they may live!

John Galsworthy

Amateur Birdwatching

Birdwatching requires very little equipment: binoculars, a bird identification guide and a notebook to jot down your observations: date, the names of species spotted, the location they were spotted in, etc.

A few tips for beginners:

- Learn to identify the plants and trees in specific regions; this will make it easier to find nesting birds.
- Stay as still as you can when birdwatching and avoid quick or abrupt movements.
- Use your binoculars to scan the scenery slowly.
- Approach birds from the side, not head on, which will scare them away.
- If you aren't alone, be careful not to talk to your companions; if you do, you'll miss wonderful opportunities to see the bird of your dreams.

Useful Web sites:

www.birdwatching.com
www.birdsofna.org

Gulls: Facts and Figures

When inland, gulls live on small rodents, grasshoppers caught in flight, worms, grubs and other insects picked up in freshly plowed fields. They catch fish and scavenge along beaches of large bodies of water. Gulls occasionally eat the eggs of cormorants and other associated nesting species. When catching fish, they splash in from a low hover but never fully immerse themselves. They are able to seize insects on the wing. At low tide they walk in the tidal flats and eat crustaceans and mollusks.

The gull's loud, raucous, mewing cry can be quite high-pitched.

Gulls usually nest in colonies on islands or shores of freshwater lakes associated with terns, cormorants, and ducks. Their nests are about 12 inches across and are made of weeds, grasses, and debris stacked on bare or rocky ground, rarely in low trees.

When one gull snatches up a fish or crab from the river, another gull will often follow it, making soft begging sounds. Once on the land, or dock, that bird will circle the gull with the food and bob its head and body up and down, softly crying and begging for some food.

Gulls are intelligent, watchful, and highly social animals.

The ring-billed gull is 18-20" high, with a wingspan of about 48". Its flight speed ranges from 11 to 43 miles per hour.

Claudia's Cornish Hens

- 4 Cornish hens
- 1 onion, coarsely chopped
- 1 celery stalk, finely chopped
- 1¹/₂ cups/150 g long-grain rice, cooked and cooled
- ¹/₂ cup/100 g seedless green grapes, halved
- ¹/₂ teaspoon oregano
- salt and pepper to taste
- ¹/₄ cup/50 g melted butter

1. Preheat oven to 400°F/215°C.
2. Under running water, wash hens three times.
3. Mix together the rice, oregano, onion, celery, raisins, salt and pepper.
4. Stuff the hens with the mixture and stitch the cavity closed.
5. Brush hens with melted butter.
6. Place hens in a shallow, ovenproof dish and roast for approximately 1 hour, basting regularly.
7. Serve with steamed and peppered fennel quarters.

Remember Claudia, the Cardinal's friend? Gossips loved to call her a bird-brain, but the little lovebird was a real Cordon Bleu in the kitchen, so make a point of trying her recipe.

Homemade Bird Feeders for Winter Feasting

Several different kinds of bird feeders are available in specialized stores, but for do-it-yourselfers, building a homemade bird feeder is as simple as 1-2-3. A pine cone can easily be transformed into a bird feeder. Wrap a bit of string around the top of the cone, then dip it in suet. For a well-balanced meal, roll the suet-covered cone in birdseed. Tie it to a high branch, well out of reach of your favourite cats and other predators. And don't forget to check the bird feeder regularly to make sure it's full. Your feathered friends are counting on you!

Caution: Birds are living things too!

It can be great fun to watch an American robin hunting for food on your lawn, but be careful not to load your grass with herbicides or pesticides. Such products are harmful to your winged dinner guests. A lovely carpet of flawless green grass may be nice to look at, but how pleasant can it be if it kills off every sign of life?

"A night of love, elusive,
Somewhere between two Sundays,
Like a large black bird
Whose wings are white."

P.-J. Toulet

Of Birds and Humans

"The flesh is sad, alas!
And I have read every book.
To flee! To flee elsewhere!
I feel the rapture of the birds
As they dream of the unfamiliar sea foam
and the endless skies."

Mallarmé

"The poet is much like birds in transit
Who build no nests on the shore
Who take not time to rest on the branch;
Nonchalantly rocked on the current's waves,
They travel, singing,
far from coasts, and the world
Knows nothing of them
save the sound of their voices."

Lamartine

Sleepy time?

There is life here:
Feathers in the eiderdown
Down in the pillows
I can hear the birds trilling:
Sleepy, oh so sleepy,
Come lay yourself down.

L.T.

I know not what small winter birds these are,
Warbling their hearts out in that dusky glade
While the pale lustre of the morning star
     In heaven begins to fade.

Not me they sing for, this —
     earth's shortest — day,
A human listening at his window-glass;
They would, affrighted, cease and flit away
     At glimpse even of my face.

And yet how strangely mine their music seems,
As if of all things loved my heart was heir,
Had helped create them — albeit in my dreams —
     And they disdained my share.

Walter de la Mare

"Even when the bird walks,
one can sense that it has wings."

Lemaître

Did you know that...

... according to one legend, the swan sings only once: just before its death.

... a "swan song" is an artist's or poet's last work.

... the rooster symbolizes vigilance.

... throughout the Celtic lands, the heron, stork or crane is mythologically associated with the creation of life; it is an elusive bird which is said to appear or disappear at will and to be guardian of all the secrets of life.

... legend has it that Aeschylus met his death when an eagle mistook his bald head for a rock and dropped a tortoise on it.

... Virgil was known as the Swan of Mantoua.

... "inseparables" are tiny Australian parrots that can survive only by living as couples.

... a project that is set aside indefinitely is described as "pigeonholed".

... ornithophobia is the fear of birds.

Swan Lake

Are you familiar with the story behind this ballet classic inspired by the music of Tchaikovsky?

Act I: At his castle, Prince Siegfried is celebrating his 21st birthday with his friends. His mother arrives and reminds him that he must choose a bride from among the ladies invited to the ball the following day. The party continues, but Siegfried stands apart, overcome by a vague melancholy. He sees some white swans fly overhead and decides to go hunt them.

Act II: At the banks of a moonlit lake near the castle, a group of swan-maidens appears. The prince has already aimed his bow when the Swan Queen presents herself and tells Siegfried that she is the Princess Odette changed into a swan, like her companions, by the sorcerer Rothbart, a spell from which she can only be freed by one who will swear eternal love to her. Now deeply in love, Siegfried swears he loves Odette and invites her to the ball, then dawn breaks and the swan-maidens are all turned back into swans.

Act III: At the ball the prince dances with six young ladies. Then, Baron Rothbart and his daughter Odile, the evil double of Odette, arrive. Siegfried decides that she is Odette, his beloved, dances with her, and publicly declares her his bride. Rothbart and his daughter leave in triumph. Then Siegfried sees the white spirit of Odette momentarily at the window and rushes to the lake.

Act IV: There the swans dance sadly as they wait for Odette. When she arrives in tears she falls to the ground; Siegfried finds her and lifts her tenderly; she is dying. He takes her tiara and throws it into the lake, which rises to submerge them both. Their spirits fly upwards towards the sky above the lake, which is calm once again.

Leda And The Swan

A sudden blow: the great wings beating still
Above the staggering girl, her thighs caressed
By the dark webs, her nape caught in his bill,
He holds her helpless breast upon his breast.

How can those terrified vague fingers push
The feathered glory from her loosening thighs?
And how can body, laid in that white rush,
But feel the strange heart beating where it lies?

A shudder in the loins engenders there
The broken wall, the burning roof and tower
And Agamemnon dead.

Being so caught up,
So mastered by the brute blood of the air,
Did she put on his knowledge with his power
Before the indifferent beak could let her drop?

William Butler Yeats, 1923

Did you know that...

When Spring arrives, the North American prairie rooster woos its very independent-minded female counterpart by ruffling its own neck feathers, revealing a portion of the underlying skin, that then swells and hangs down on both sides of its face. The bag-like structure is filled with air and the rooster empties it to emit a loud snoring noise, much like the sound of a bagpipe. Its mating call can be heard from more than half a mile away.

Native North American Indian tribes invented their rhythmic and energy-charged dances by looking to the wild rooster for inspiration.

In Canada, on Bonaventure Island in the Gaspé region, late June marks the arrival of some 25,000 garnet couples, who build nests using algae, mud and twigs. This bird colony is one of only two in the entire world, the other being located on Saint Kilda Island on the coast of Scotland and totalling some 40,000 birds.

The lead sinkers used by fishers are a threat for several species of wild aquatic birds who swallow them accidentally. The birds in jeopardy include the loon, the swan, the great blue heron, the cormorant and the pelican. There are several fishing items that are lead-free, using alternative materials such as bismuth, pewter, copper, stainless steel and a compound composed of polypropylene and tungsten.

Pasta and Turkey Salad, Grand Duke Style

- 2 cups/500 ml cooked turkey, cubed
- 3 cups/750 ml wholewheat shell or bowtie-shaped pasta
- 2 onions, chopped finely
- $1/2$ red pepper, thinly sliced
- $1/2$ green pepper, thinly sliced
- 1 can mandarin oranges
- $1/4$ cup/60 ml roasted pine nuts

- $3/4$ cup/125 ml mayonnaise
- $3/4$ cup/125 ml plain yogurt
- 1 tablespoon/5 g curry powder
- 1 tablespoon/5 g paprika
- salt and pepper to taste

1. Cook pasta *al dente*, rinse under cold water and drain.
2. Mix pasta with turkey, onions, peppers and mandarin oranges.
3. In a bowl, mix together the yogurt, mayonnaise, curry, paprika, and salt and pepper.
4. Add the preparation to the pasta and turkey mixture and blend.
5. Garnish with pine nuts and serve.

Claudia doesn't cook very often, but when she does decide to venture into the kitchen, she prepares her dishes with style and flair. She loves to linger over her culinary masterpieces, savouring each bite tête-à-tête with the Cardinal, alias the Grand Duke of Mongolia.

A Gift from Heaven

One morning in December, as I sat alone eating my breakfast in an underground café in a rather dull and gray skyscraper, Life brought me a gift that brightened my whole day and created a fond memory that will last a lifetime. To my astonishment, a tiny sparrow alighted on the empty chair opposite mine. Methodically, it began to clean its feathers. Since it was very early in the morning and the usual horde of workers hadn't yet arrived, I had the opportunity to watch the proceedings for a good while: the bird wriggled about, lifting one wing at a time, using its beak to comb each feather until it was silky smooth once again.

Fascinated by its assurance and the speed of its movements, I was careful not to move, for fear of frightening it away. But the small creature come to keep me company seemed oblivious to the world. Its focus was the task at hand and it was very, very careful not to let a single feather go untouched.

My sparrow bent its head, used it to explore the underside of a wing. It ruffled its feathers, scratched a spot or two, smoothed, untangled a few knots, then went through the entire routine on the opposite side of its fragile body. Last but not least, its minuscule breast was the object of its careful attention.

The ceremony lasted ten or twelve minutes — as long as the morning calm allowed and until other breakfast-seekers made an appearance and my winged friend went on its way. I hadn't noticed where it had come from and I didn't see where it went. I had the distinct impression that it was the only sparrow living in this dark basement dwelling, far from fresh water and lush greenery, but no doubt I was wrong. Life and the living have resources that, for most of us, go unnoticed all too often.

L.T.

The Eagle

I have been to the end of the earth.
I have been to the end of the waters.
I have been to the end of the sky.
I have been to the end of the mountains.
I have found none that are not my friends.

Navajo proverb

"Oh, Eagle, come with wings outspread
in sunny skies.
Oh, Eagle, come and bring us peace,
thy gentle peace.
Oh, Eagle, come and give new life
to us who pray."

Pawnee Prayer

"In an eagle there is all the wisdom of the world."

Minnicoujou saying

ear and yet so far and unattainable, you've dreamed of spreading y[our]
wn wings, of soaring, of letting the wind lift you far into the sky, on eth[er]
al routes free of any obstacle, on routes providing a magnificent view o[f]
f earth's countless beauties. What a wonderful dream! What a wonde[r]
ul sense of weightlessness! What wonderful freedom! From the tin[y]
ummingbird to the mightiest eagle, from the brightest plumed to the maj[esti]
cally black, birds are among the most wondrous and beautiful creatu[res]

es. What a wonderful dream! What a wonderful sense of weightlessne[ss]
What wonderful freedom! From the tiniest hummingbird to the might[iest]
agle, from the brightest plumed to the majestically black, birds are am[ong]
e most wondrous and beautiful creatures on our planet. We look
em for the pleasure they bring to our eyes, we study them to underst[and]
eir behavior, we use them as a source of inspiration to reach highe[r]
each further. It comes as no surprise that birds have inspired so
any of our poets and song writers. Words and lyrics that speak of f[...]
re common in every human language. The human's fascination